THE UPLAND EQUATION

Books by Charles Fergus

SHADOW CATCHER

A ROUGH-SHOOTING DOG

GUN DOG BREEDS

THE WINGLESS CROW

THE UPLAND EQUATION

A Modern Bird Hunter's Code

CHARLES FERGUS

Lyons & Burford, Publishers

Printed in the United States of America

10 9 8 7 6 5 4 3 2 1

Design by M.R.P.

Library of Congress Cataloging-in-Publication Data

Fergus, Charles.
    The upland equation : a modern bird hunter's code / Charles
Fergus.
        p.   cm.
    ISBN 1-55821-363-5 (cloth)
    1. Upland game bird shooting—East (U.S.)   I. Title.
SK323.F46   1995
799.2'42'0974—dc20   95-12399
                                                                              CIP

To my mother and father,
who, if they did not completely understand
why their son wanted to hunt,
nonetheless let him discover himself.

CONTENTS

All the sounds of this valley run together into one great echo, a song that is sung by all the spirits of this valley. Only a hunter hears it.

—CHAIM POTOK
I Am the Clay

FOREWORD

Twenty-five years ago, struggling to reclaim a heritage of bird hunting interrupted by the generational struggles of the sixties, I wrote a letter to M. R. Montgomery, then the staff outdoor writer for the *Boston Globe.* How, I asked, could I learn the skills and traditions of the upland shooting life? Monty replied with a column, the title and sense of which was "Find yourself a gentleman with a dog."

It was good advice, and served me well; I'd still give it to any young (or beginning) bird hunter whom I could not take afield myself. In matters like hunting and fishing and falconry, mentors are priceless. They teach you nuance, and detail, and what is really important. A "gentleman" (or, nowadays, "gentlewoman") with a dog is likely to know just that. They know, through the dog's senses, how the birds behave, where they are likely to be, and whether they will hold or flush wild. Because they have a dog, they have (I hope) learned to be gentle, to listen to an animal. With a little luck, this in turn has taught them to listen to other things—the birds, the wind and weather, small mammals; and to use their other senses—sight, smell, and touch. Ideally, such feedback will make them think about such matters as what guns and loads are appropriate. They will learn game cookery in order both to make the most of wonderful meat and, more abstractly, to treat their quarry with the utmost respect. They will probably become serious conservationists, and wonder and worry about matters like the decline of woodcock on the flightlines of the east. They will become rooted in their choosen country.

Charles Fergus is a gentleman with a dog, his springer Jenny, rooted in the hill country of Central Pennsylvania. He listens to her (I once called his earlier book, *A Rough-Shooting Dog,* the story of a love affair between a man and his dog). He listens to birds and mammals and weather. "Feedback," for lack of a better word, has taught him the virtues of English shotguns. Although he is far from a rich man, he'll tell you how he went to England to find an affordable gun that also pleased him esthetically. Be warned: he is likely to convince you to try the same. As another gentleman with a gun, Datus Proper, put it, "There are those of us who need all the help we can get, plus a parable on hunting." He knows that bird hunting demands real wild birds, the partnership of a dog, a gun that works with you, and the knowledge of mortality.

Yeah, that too: the heavy stuff. Fergus says, and I agree: "... hunters owe it to themselves to try to understand what it is that urges them out. To fail to examine the source of the hunting instinct is to fail to experience it fully. It is too simple to say it is good experience, or pleasant pastime, or exciting sport, or even a means of experiencing nature. It is those things and more; it is about learning to be patient, giving thanks, becoming a child again. It is about facing death, and living life as fully as one can." Serious? Yes, but never solemn or joyless, only (appropriately) thoughtful. Fergus knows that "hunting is seeking for beauty, a beauty that is embodied in the land and the game, in the gun, and also in the dog." And unless you are like the writer he mentions in his introduction, who "considered the making of maple syrup and the growing of potatoes to be quaint, remnant tasks," you are bound to enjoy his perceptions. (If you *are* like that writer, perhaps you should read *The Upland Equation* as a corrective!)

In short, Charles Fergus is not only "a gentleman with a dog" but as sound a guide as you will ever find to introduce you to the joys of country, bird, dog, and gun. If you don't have your own mentor, he will take you in hand, with grace and wisdom. Even if you do have a mentor (or are one), you should read this book. Your mentor will probably enjoy it too.

Steve Bodio
Bozeman, MT
Spring 1995

A friend of mine liked to say that bird hunting, for him, had three requisites: Game, on land that was ample and healthy enough to support it. A dog in synchrony with its master and the birds. And a gun that gave pleasure both to shoot and to behold.

My friend is gone now, and by the time he neared the end of his life he had only the land—the uplands of central Pennsylvania—and the shotgun, a scarred, brush-silvered L. C. Smith, fondly referred to as "Elsie." He often reminisced about his dogs, in particular one setter with an uncanny ability to read cover, work with her master, and anticipate the behavior of their favorite quarry, the ruffed grouse.

My friend, I believe, was a wise man. I have come to think of his three elements—game, dog, and gun—as the upland equation; actually, as one half of an equation that is balanced by—and that brings into balance—the human element, the hunter. Pursuing this state of excited equilibrium has placed me among wild creatures in their natural surroundings. It has lured and challenged me. It has helped determine where I live; even, to some extent, the career I follow.

Recently I read in *The New Yorker* an obituary for the writer Berton Roueché, who was recalled as having composed, among other things, "a series of sparkling pieces about people who were left over from the nineteenth century—rural people who made maple syrup or grew potatoes." Apparently the obituary writer considered the making of maple syrup and the growing of potatoes to be quaint, remnant tasks. I wonder where he or she believes maple syrup and potatoes come from. I also wonder what the writer would think of a person who hunted. A person who roamed through the thickets, pursuing and killing wild birds, then taking them home, cleaning and cooking them, and—with great gustatory pleasure—eating them. I am sure that hunting is considered even more outdated (and, by many, more reprehensible) than tapping sugar maples or cultivating spuds: something practiced by recidivists left over from a century even dimmer and more distant than the one most recently past.

I cannot say that I am writing for naive modernists. I am more comfortable talking to people with an outdoor bent, be they hunters or those who are simply curious about why other folk might hunt. I do know that I want to examine, ever more deeply, the perceptions and joys—the essential sense of belonging and balance—that hunting brings to me.

This book will deal with bird hunting in the Eastern uplands, a tradition and a place long celebrated by sporting writers. I feel fortunate to live in this part of the world, with its diverse vegetation and wildlife, its varying weathers and distinct seasons. For others, the upland equation may differ slightly: They may cherish the game and land beneath the reaching sky of the Great Plains; in the arroyos and brittle mountains of the Southwest; in the pine flatwoods and old field openings of Dixie; in the hills and cedar bogs Down East. Their dogs may be of a different size, color, and function than mine. They may have different ideas as to what constitutes a proper shotgun. Yet there will be shared elements. They will understand, as I do, that were it not for the game and the land it inhabits, there would be no hunt. Were it not for the dog—its eagerness, its nose for the birds—the connection between human and game would be disjunct. Were it not for the gun, there would be no stately dance.

I hunt often, and with great pleasure. I hunt for the game, the dog, and the gun. I hunt to be myself.

1

THE GAME

My home is in the uplands of central Pennsylvania. All my life I have lived on the western edge of what the state Topographic and Geologic Survey calls the "Appalachian Mountain Section of the Valley and Ridge Province." Here, long parallel ridges stand between broad fertile valleys, the ridges and valleys running generally from northeast to southwest (most useful in keeping one's bearings). Although we know them as mountains, the ridges are more like rugged hills; capped with sandstone, they are generally dry, but those with large, flattened summits often accommodate small streams, called "runs," that meander to the slopes, then rattle their way down through rocky gaps. Springs punctuate the mountainsides, seeping down to the valleys. In places the valleys swallow the streams, forcing them to run along underground for some distance, in fissures within the limestone bedrock. Ultimately, though, the streams emerge to trellis the valleys with their curving and meandering forms. They join and become creeks, flow through age-old notches they have carved in the mountains, and debouch into rivers named Juniata and Susquehanna. Along the waters are bogs, marshes, oxbows, and backwaters.

Trees cloak the ridges: oak, ash, maple, hickory, black gum, white pine, hemlock, and dozens of others, each with its distinctive silhouette, bark texture, nuts or fruits, and autumn colors; each to me as familiar and constant as an old friend. Some of the bigger ridges are Tussey Mountain, Stone Mountain, Blacklog Mountain, Shade Mountain, Jacks Mountain, and Tuscarora Mountain. In places, the ridges twist together and interweave in forested complication. Some of the ridges have two names, one on the map (Bald Eagle Mountain) and one on the tongues of long-time locals (Muncy Mountain, since the landform rises in the north near the river town of Muncy, where the Susquehanna makes its great bend south toward the Chesapeake). Muncy Mountain, under whose wooded brow I hunt, continues south for many miles: I have heard that it runs all the way to Alabama, an oceanic swell of upland, but I have never explored the truth of that statement, even on maps, because I am a provincial man, and my province is central Pennsylvania.

Here are towns, some neat and prosperous, others shabby and poor, and a small city that is sprawling out with alarming quickness. Outside the municipalities lie woodlots, riparian woods, intensively farmed land, fields that are reverting to brush, bogs, beaver ponds, a few small lakes, and extensive mountain forests. Within this range of habitats can be found mourning doves, pheasants, woodcock, and ruffed grouse. Ducks and geese live along the waters.

Aldo Leopold once wrote, "Everybody knows that the autumn landscape in the north woods is the land, plus a red maple, plus a ruffed grouse. In terms of conventional physics, the grouse represents only a millionth of either the mass or the energy of an acre. Yet subtract the grouse and the whole thing is dead."

The land comes alive through its wild creatures. I come to know the land through hunting the birds. Hunting has opened the earth to me and let me sense the rhythms and hierarchies of nature.

The end of October and the beginning of November are the golden days. There is something magical about this time of year. Leaves still cling and show their colors, but signs of winter are manifold—bare branches, cold rain, geese wobbling across a cloud-smudged sky. Magic also resides in the fact that I never know precisely when the woodcock will be in. I know, roughly, where to find them: in the damp lands next to the creek, in the old cow pastures, in the low-lying brushy tracts. Our valley has its share of such cover, and if I visit it often enough I can usually raise some birds. First I spot their white gooey droppings (like melted marshmallows) decorating the fallen leaves or bare earth. Then my springer spaniel, Jenny, gets her tail going like mad, with little nasal whufflings amid her quick panting. Finally the woodcock themselves, a first sonorous fluttering-up that can provoke a too-quick shot, the bird carrying on into the cover. I like to pause after that initial flush and miss—bring Jenny to heel, though she is fiery to go on—and stand there for a moment, anticipating the hunt to come.

Many modern folk do not know what a woodcock is. I myself was unsure when, at the age of sixteen, I spied a pair of them squatting beneath a sumac clump. The woodcock is a chunky bird about the size of a fist: short pert tail, long skinny bill, big buttonlike eyes set well back in the sides of the head. Owing to the positioning of its eyes, a woodcock is able to see laterally and behind itself with more acuity than to the front.

Dogs react strongly to woodcock scent, and usually the bird crouches passively, which lets a pointing dog work in close. I particularly enjoy hunting woodcock with my friend Nick. His black-and-white setter weaves through the brush, bell tinkling hopefully. We stroll along behind, talking softly, shotguns broken over our arms. When the tintinnabulation stops, we click the guns shut, and, hearts thumping, home in on the frozen dog.

The actual shooting can be easy, can be hard. Sometimes a woodcock will flush, then flutter onward in straight and simple flight; even if shot at and missed, it may alight within a few rods. That could be a wing-weary migrant who came in with the dawn, having flown eighty miles in the night. Give it a day's rest, and it will offer greater challenge.

For woodcock I use number 8 shot, which are very small pellets, to give a dense, uniform pattern. Nevertheless, I am humbled by woodcock frequently. What complicates the wing-shooting is the bird's evasive flight (like a bat, quickly this way, then that) and the stiff cover it inhabits (devil's club, crab apple, thornapple, blackberry, haw; the low dog-hair stuff overtopped with maple, musclewood, aspen, alder, pine). Last fall I watched one of my friends, a superb wingshot, utterly defeated by a woodcock that spiraled upward in front of his barrels, broke back over his head, sideslipped behind an aspen's crown, dipped down and twittered off about five feet above the ground.

If I kill a woodcock, Jenny fetches it. She comes padding back, her eyes on mine, her tail wagging low; often a russet wing wobbles beneath her jaw. Kneeling, I feel like an archaeologist who has unearthed an ancient talisman whose decorative painted surface somehow remains intact. Black horizontal barring crosses the domed head. Pale cinnamon plumage cloaks the breast and sides, underlain with gray-black down. The bird's back is patterned with numerous browns—russet, umber, ochre, sepia—in a pattern as beautiful as it is complex. The bill is often flecked with mud—an outsize appendage with a sandpapery undersurface to the upper mandible, and a long rugose tongue, for securing slippery worms. Like me, the woodcock hunts for its meat.

Sometimes the coverts are full of woodcock. Sometimes we kill them as ancillary prey when hunting grouse. I am told that fewer and fewer woodcock channel through the Eastern uplands each fall. The main reason, I suspect, is that their habitat is diminishing, from human development and from the maturation of brushland into forest. (The woodcock cannot live in mature woods.) Perhaps hunting is at least partly responsible. Despite statistics charting the woodcock's decline, the New England states continue to have long seasons. In neighboring Ohio, the state wildlife commission lets hunters shoot woodcock for nine weeks and take five birds per day. By contrast, here in Pennsylvania the season has been shortened to two weeks, with a daily limit of three. (All right, I would like a somewhat longer season. Last year, the weather was mild and the flights out of the north were delayed, and for the last three weeks in November—when woodcock were forbidden and I had turned to grouse—it was hard explaining to Jenny why, when she flushed a woodcock, I couldn't shoot at it.)

Because the woodcock is shy, and because wildlife biologists have not conducted much research on it (woodcock not being as crowd-pleasing as wild turkeys or deer), we do not fully understand the species, the ins and outs of its reproduction and migration, the rumored shiftings of birds here on the breeding grounds before they depart for the southern wintering range. In Mississippi and Louisiana, where most of the continent's woodcock spend the winter, hunters are increasingly turning from quail (quail numbers are falling as *their* habitat is consumed by industrial agriculture and urban sprawl) to woodcock, with long seasons and liberal bag limits on the long-billed bird.

If the woodcock were lost from our pantheon of game birds, the upland equation might not be capable of balancing. As it is, I savor the short, sweet season and feel little disappointment when, my gun barrels trickling smoke, a 'cock flies off swerving through the brush.

Two of the reasons I hunt ducks are the time of day they draw me out (dawn, often with a fiery sunrise) and the places they take me: the bogs fringing the lakes, the streams that vein the land and carry its life's blood back to the source. Sometimes on rainy, howly days I go ducking: Had I planned to pursue grouse or woodcock, the weather would have kept me indoors. But ducks are active in bad weather; the worse it seems to me, the more they like it.

Hunting waterfowl, I usually employ a technique called "jump-shooting." This is a literal term: Sneaking through places where ducks dwell, I try to get them to jump from the water so that I can get a shot. Jump-shooting does not require decoys or a boat. One does not have to sit in a blind, garbed in bulky clothing, and, despite being so bundled, fidget from the cold. Meandering, one is apt to see wondrous things: herons in stiltish, gawky repose or tucked-up, waltz-like flight; beavers who slap their tails on the water and dive; ospreys grappling with fish. There are odd plants such as spatterdock, bog cotton, bulrushes, sphagnum, and cranberry (finding a nice patch of cranberries, I'll drink off the water in my jug and fill it with the ruddy, pebble-like fruit; at home, it makes into a fine relish to go with roast duck).

Compared with the other upland birds, I use large shot—6's for jump shooting, 3's if the chances are long—to pierce the ducks' stiff feathers and thick down. I use a shotgun that I don't mind getting muddy or banged up. Some duck hunters go whole hog and buy special boats and dozens of decoys and fancy camouflage suits, but I prefer a more modest approach. Normally I shoot around half a dozen ducks a year, which is enough. The main enjoyment, in addition to duck stir-frys, is wandering through the mucky places where they dwell.

Clad in hipboots, I hunt by walking slowly along the creeks and streams, veering off into the brush and sneaking up on quiet backwaters. A lake near my home can attract up to a dozen different species, including blue-winged teal (about the size of a barn pigeon: they spring from the water as if catapulted and buzz past so fast I often can't get off a shot); mallards (big ducks with lots of succulent meat on their bones); wood ducks with their swept-back crested heads and (in the males; the females are cryptically dull) eery carmine eyes and neon-bright plumage colors; and occasionally even canvasbacks (grand heavy fellows that run along on the top of the water to get enough lift for takeoff).

I remember a hunt from last fall. Jenny and I slipped down a remote upland valley at first light. Frost lay in the swales, and a thin layer of mist floated above the water, a stream above the stream. We came to where the rivulet crossed a meadow and curved through a stand of oaks; beneath the trees, acorns lay scattered on the ground.

The ducks were off the pool and away through the woods before I could raise the gun. Wood ducks, a pair, shadowy enough that I half-questioned whether I had even seen them until I heard the ripples lapping against the bank. The ducks had flown downstream ahead of us. The oaks gave way to another meadow; keeping to the stream, we entered a bowl overgrown with alders, wizened trees with twisted, blackish branches and fruits like little pine cones. Beaver ponds strung through the alders like silver beads on a bracelet. No sound, save for my legs swishing through the water, splashings and snortings from the spaniel.

It came from behind me: the whistling of wings. I raised the gun and swiveled at the waist. As the gray forms disappeared behind the alders, I cheeked the stock and pulled the trigger. Amid the echoes of the shot, I heard a splash. Jenny churned across the pond, lunged through the alders, and swam on. A single duck circled high overhead. I stood contemplating the dull sky, the luminous colors all around—the rich purple-red of the huckleberry, pale gray boulders flecked with orange and green lichen, the remnant yellows and reds glowing from the hills. Finally Jenny came paddling back. Pond weeds decorated her head. Her eyes, as always, were fixed on mine, and between her jaws was the duck.

Four, five, six quick beats of their long, raked-back wings—the body arrowing through the air—then the wings clasped at the side for a shimmering instant—then the feverish pumping again: Doves are the most agile of our game birds, and the fastest. Doves can materialize as gray specks on the horizon and, moments later, be flashing past. As they whip by, their wings whistling, I glimpse gold and lavender hints in the subtle gray-buff plumage, and white margins along the pointed tail.

The mourning dove is named for the male's solemn call: five to seven cooing notes, the second pitched higher than the rest, drawn out and richly plaintive, like a recorder played soft and low. The dove is classified as a songbird in several states, protected from hunting though it need not be. Its population in the past century has mushroomed. Mourning doves nest in towns and suburbs as well as in rural areas. They thrive in intensively cultivated places from which other species have vanished. They eat weed seeds, some scarcely larger than pepper grains (single doves have been found having six thousand seeds of foxtail grass in their crops), as well as corn, wheat, and oats left by the harvesters. A pair of doves will raise two young in a twig nest that looks as if they threw it together in minutes; over the summer, they may bring off five broods. Doves are a challenge to the wingshooter and a delight to the epicurean.

When I think of dove hunting, I think of sweating, carrying extra water for the dog, squinting into the sky's glare, watching monarch butterflies waft past in their leisurely southward migration, being bored (when the shooting lags) into contemplating small dull rocks and the spider-shaped support roots of cornstalks—then startling at approaching "doves" that turn out to be kestrels, swallows, and wasps (I have to blink several times to restore my depth perception). Dove season, arriving as it does in early September, is a preamble to the other types of upland gunning. The hunter, camouflaged, must lurk in the corn or the weeds. In the instant that the hunter stands and raises the gun, a passing dove can flare to one side, spill the air from its wings and drop, or pour on the speed (or perform all of these maneuvers in sequence). The bird weighs but four to five ounces, about twice the weight of a shotshell, and I will usually expend two shells before dropping a dove with the third. (Sometimes the ratio is worse.) A good thing about hunting doves is the number of shots, both simple and complicated, that you may get on an outing. It is intensely exciting to watch a dove approaching from a long ways off, to wait until the last moment, pop up from your hideout, sweep the gun and snap the shot, and see the bird stopped suddenly in a feathery puff. My friend Carl, a practiced, excellent wingshot, once killed the day's limit of twelve doves with twelve shots—he got so nervous about his last two attempts that he let several difficult doves pass while waiting for closer targets. Even in my wildest dreams I never believe I can down that straight dozen.

One afternoon we posted on the edge of some mowed alfalfa—spiced with weed seeds, usually a good draw—and got scarcely a shot. The few birds we did bring down had wheat kernels in their crops. All afternoon the doves streamed overhead, out of shooting range and bound for some distant realm. Finally Carl got into the car. After searching for a while, he found their hub: a failed wheatfield that the farmer had mown down. Carl quickly located the farmer and got permission to hunt. He came back and picked us up. We drove to the field, stepped out of the car, and gawked.

It was a scene from the Alfred Hitchcock movie, *The Birds*. No sound and very little motion came from the massed doves, only a slight shuffling of hunched gray bodies and, in the foreground, the raising of hundreds of heads. A pair of marsh hawks coursed the far end of the field, causing bursts of doves to fly off in panic. One in our party, a wildlife biologist experienced at waterfowl surveys, counted the birds on one part of the field, extrapolated, and said that at least two thousand doves were feeding in the stubble, with almost that many on an adjoining plowed field.

We scattered—Carl to an errant line of corn jutting into the field, Jerry to beneath a scraggly walnut from which a dozen doves fled at his approach. I stamped down a circle in a patch of knee-high weeds, in a swale the farmer hadn't cut. I walked out into the field and set down decoys—hollow plastic doves—which in retrospect seems laughingly unnecessary. Doves arrived and landed in waves as I was positioning the decoys on the ground. Noticing me, they fluttered up, shifted over a hundred yards or so, and set back down. I returned to my spot, loaded my gun, and knelt.

While we nicked away at the near edges (like the marsh hawks slowly making their rounds), flock after flock swept into the field and left again in regular waves. The birds flew no slower for being so numerous, but I actually shot rather well. When Jenny ran out for a retrieve, doves that I hadn't even seen landing jumped up from the weedy stubble and flashed off. It was over in less than an hour: Next to a pile of spent cartridges lay a mound of twelve doves. Jenny, gray feathers sticking to her lips, sat quivering and panting, lashing her tail, waiting for another retrieve. Her amber eyes reflected the silhouettes of doves, dozens of doves, flickering overhead.

The ring-necked pheasant is not native to Pennsylvania, or to anywhere else in North America. It comes from Asia and has been transplanted around the world, chiefly by people who wanted to hunt it. The pheasant that lives in Pennsylvania is thought to derive from cross-breedings between Chinese pheasants, Mongolian pheasants, Japanese pheasants, and English pheasants (themselves descendants of a race from the Caucasus region near the Caspian Sea).

Two decades ago, pheasants were plentiful across the

Northeast, apparently well integrated with the land and the other wild creatures. They lived in the brushy verges of farm fields, lending an air of exotic wildness to the cultivated places. When pressed, they would hide in deep thickets and cattail swamps. In the early nineteen seventies, when I was beginning to hunt, the upland farms had healthy populations of wild pheasants—even if I wasn't a good enough shot to bag very many of them. Nowadays, we have few wild pheasants. Perhaps it is because farmers mow their alfalfa fields earlier than before, smashing the hens' nests. In managing their holdings to permit the use of larger tractors, farmers have grubbed out fencerows, eliminated thickets, and drained marshes that once sheltered the birds. One undeniable force in the pheasants' decline is the loss of natural land to the hunters' bane of houses, roads, and shopping malls.

Most of the pheasants I kill are "stocked" birds—raised in pens and set loose before the season by the state game commission. I tramp into a grouse or a woodcock cover, Jenny skids into some hot scent, she works the trail for twenty or forty yards (I keep up with her, my excitement mounting)—until a pheasant gives a ringing, insulted cackle as it vaults from the undergrowth. The shooting is not as difficult as it is with the native game birds—all swifter, shiftier fliers—but the pheasant represents a stimulation, a test. On the first day of pheasant season I report to a public hunting area, where I compete with scores of other orange-clad hunters (like fishermen on opening day, cheek-to-jowl along the creeks), and, thanks to my spaniel, usually bag my two-bird allotment. By midmorning we are toiling up some lonesome slope for grouse.

I remember a day, before I had Jenny, when I tracked a pheasant in half an inch of snow, around and through a two-acre patch. Alders, a trickling stream, waist-high goldenrod, wild rose—I followed with shotgun at the ready, reading the tracks, scanning the snow-dusted weeds. I strode ahead quickly; I kept looping out in front, trying to intercept. I must have made four circuits around the patch before finally trapping my quarry where the brush petered out into open woods. He went up cackling, as beautiful in his varicolored plumage as a clutch of released balloons. He tried to swoop back over me, to regain the thick cover. How well I remember the rush of triumph I felt when I brought him down cleanly.

For the best in pheasant hunting (the best we have in Pennsylvania; I have heard about pheasant hunting in the Midwest and the Great Plains, and what we have here does not compare), I travel downstate. Carl and I hunt for wild ringnecks near his home—although I am sure we also encounter some stocked birds along with the wild ones. After the crops are cut, we seek out small pockets of cover (which seem to grow smaller and fewer each year). All, it seems, are within sight—and, more's the pity, within sound—of quarries, highways, and new four-hundred-thousand-dollar houses. (It is incongruous to hear a tractor-trailer accelerating, a lawnmower blathering, or a football game played on some weekend tinkerer's radio, when hieing your dog into game cover.)

One day last November, we worked through twenty acres of foxtails, goldenrod, Johnson grass, and mulberry, an oasis of cover in a desert of sliced-off cornstubble and picked soybean stems.

Carl's Labrador retriever hurried to the fore, darted right, then left, and drove up a long-tailed rooster. The bird flew toward me. I watched Carl as I watched the pheasant. I saw him twitch his shotgun toward his shoulder, then stop it—as I had known he would, in consideration of my safety. I turned to my left and raised my own gun, thinking to kill the bird as it quartered past. When I pulled the trigger, the pheasant did not falter. So surprised was I at missing that I failed to fire the second barrel. The pheasant cleared a hedgerow, we followed, and the bird evaded us again, flushing before we got close. A pheasant may look like a balloon when you raise it in open terrain, but let it attain speed—or be forced to watch for a few seconds before swinging into action—and you will be suitably challenged.

Physically, pheasants are the toughest of the ground-dwelling upland birds. I use large shot—number 6 or 5—to penetrate to the vitals and effect clean kills. With the possible exception of ducks, there are no other game birds that require a dog as absolutely as pheasants do, both to get the birds into the air and to track down wounded ones: Even a grievously hit ring-neck may pick itself up and run away.

In grading out the joys of the uplands, I must place pheasant hunting near the bottom. Since it is not a member of our original fauna, the pheasant lacks some of the appeal of the woodcock and the ruffed grouse, although wild pheasants (the ones raised in the weed patches and cornfields and swamps) can certainly be considered "native," much like the brown trout whose forebears, many generations ago, lived in European waters. But stocked pheasants, no matter how wary they may be, how evasive, how apparently wild, I cannot see as anything but cannon fodder. Few of them possess the savvy to survive from one year to the next. They do not spring from the land and so are not a part of it. I do not mind hunting them, I almost feel as if I *should* be hunting them since my license fee has already purchased them. But each year I seem to hunt pheasants less frequently, less zealously, than the year before.

The bird that is steadfast and always present, that lives outside my door, that is the staple of my venatic delight, is the ruffed grouse.

In the Pennsylvania uplands, grouse season opens in mid-October. It is a good but not an optimum time to hunt. Panting and sweating, one gets pricked with thorns, quirted by branches, and has spider webs plastered across one's mouth. The leaves, still thick on the trees, block one's sight. There are also crisp blue mornings, naive birds that offer close shooting, and the irresistible lure of being outdoors when fall's colors burn their brightest.

Each October, I seem to encounter at least one perching grouse. When I first started hunting, I was so concerned about filling my game pouch that I shot grouse however and whenever I could, including in trees and on the ground. However, my respect for the bird—and for the difficulty of shooting it on the wing—won out. Now when I see a rookie rubbernecking on a limb, I approach with the gun down, let the bird flash out, and attempt the shot. It is good practice, both for my wingshooting and my self-control. Often I miss, because this sequence of waiting—watching—sometimes even hollering—wreaks havoc on the instinctive wingshooting drill: facing the flush, getting the feet sorted out, swinging the gun, and reaching out for the fleeing form.

Fall edges toward winter, and another season of grouse comes on. The weather has cooled. The birds have learned the ways of hunters and dogs. The hunters have gained an advantage, too, with the leaves finally fallen. At this time, I like hunting in a misting rain. The colors are soft and muted; the scent lies close to the ground. Jenny and I tread quietly, hoping to sneak up on a bird. It is true that the hunter who makes less noise will see more (and closer) grouse.

Although November's coverts appear drab and lackluster, subtle colors remain: burgundy sumac bobs, bronze oak leaves, waxy-green crabapples, scarlet hawthorn fruit (dubbed "hawsies" by the locals), barberries and winterberries of an even fiercer red, and the delicate yellow starbursts of the witch hazel flowers. The grouse, when they flush, go out on thrumming wings, in their bronze and chestnut plumage, their black-tipped tails spread and their crests erect.

A biologist friend tells me that the typical Pennsylvania grouse hunter flushes an average of 1.5 birds per hour. I will usually put up three in an hour, and attribute my success to good coverts, a good dog, and a willingness to walk. The more ground I cover, the more grouse I flush. Which does not mean that I hunt at a constant forced march. One of the best ways to put a skulking grouse into the air is to suddenly stop: The bird thinks you have spotted him, and are preparing to pounce. The trick is to pause near a grouse (or at least near a place where you think a grouse may be skulking, which may be inferred from the behavior of your dog), and in a place that offers clear shooting.

Early in the year I use number 8 shot, the same size as for woodcock. Grouse are not tough birds, like pheasants, and one or two pellets will usually bring one down. Later I shift to $7\frac{1}{2}$'s or even 6's: fewer pellets per cartridge, but they give better penetration through the dense winter plumage.

The season of grouse that I most enjoy comes after the solstice. Often there is snow. If the snow is powdery, the birds will bed in it, and it will shield them from predators while keeping them warm. Henry David Thoreau wrote of the ruffed grouse: "What a hardy bird, born amid the dry leaves, of the same color with them, that, grown up, lodges in the snow and lives on buds and twigs!"

Last year, a foot of snow fell after Christmas, stayed, and for the longest time did not crust over. Hunting, I glided through the coves, glissaded down the slopes. The ridges and hills stood out like pale blue arms and knuckles. The air was still and cold. Icicles formed in my beard; Jenny grew ice eyebrows. She stopped frequently to chew the snow from between her pads, and I helped her by biting away the ice balls, not easily accessible to her teeth, that built up between her sides and forelegs.

With snow in the coverts, the brown birds show up well. Often in winter, four or five grouse will cluster together. Tracks mark the snow, faint ones that keep my interest high, sharp ones that set my nerves to jangling. In powder, a grouse's tracks make a broad trough; on a firmer surface, they describe a straight line, each print pointing slightly inward and with the rear toe digging a small furrow. The tracks of an unalarmed grouse potter about, from grapevine (purple stains where fallen fruit once rested), to spring seep (succulent cinquefoil leaves edging the trickling water), beneath an overhanging catbriar tangle (wicked thorns on that vine), to an habitual resting place in the lee of a log or a patch of mountain laurel (marked by a pile of curved olive-and-white droppings). When a grouse knows it is being followed, its tracks stretch far apart. Sometimes at the end of the trail, the spaniel drives the bird up from the brush. Sometimes all we find are the mute curving scratches of wingtips in the snow.

2

THE DOG

It is a sensuous thing, having a dog. The other day I was assembling a blueberry pie, wearing only boxer shorts because it was a sticky summer's evening, when the spaniel came sneaking and surprised me behind the knee with her ice-cube nose. In winter, when I lie before the fire, she curls up in the crook of my body. I kiss her shamelessly on the dome of her head. I like the smell of her fur, dry or wet. Even though she is now middle-aged (come to think of it, I qualify as well), she loves to play, barking and sparring her paws at me, catching my hand loosely in her jaws. She goes berry-picking with the rest of the family (daintily plucking fruit from the stems with her incisors; none of it making it into the berry buckets), loves riding in the canoe, and escorts me up the hill to the mailbox every noon. Having a dog is fun. A dog is a boon companion in all of those moments when you are not hunting—and a helper and comrade when you are.

Hunting is the real occupation of my dog. She knows she is a hunter. It is her life's focus. By allowing her to reveal her skill and character, it helps fulfill her. In turn, she helps fulfill me.

It is hard to describe the feeling of enrichment that comes from hunting with a good dog. Many factors are involved. The dog, with its sense of smell and its ability to cover the ground, puts the hunter into contact with more birds. It gives the gunner more and better shots: The birds, paying attention to the canine intruder, heed the hunter less. The dog fetches wounded birds that otherwise would die lingering deaths and feed only opossums and raccoons. The avidity of a bird dog is catching; the dog, descending as it does from predatory ancestors, helps us remember that we, too, descend from predators. Dogs clarify and intensify the urge in us to hunt.

I am never alone when I hunt with Jenny. I like the logistical simplicity of it: If I want to suddenly change directions and check out a certain patch of brambles because maybe, just maybe, a grouse will be there (on that south-facing slope, where the winter sun shines and the grapevines grow thick)—I just do it. I don't have to consult. I don't have to explain or justify. I give two pips on the whistle and wave my hand, and we do what the hunters' instincts tell us.

When we are working in concert, when Jenny is combing the cover in front of me, when I am watching her, looking for her tail to speed up, her coursing to become more directed; when I am listening intently for the twittering flush of a woodcock, or the thunder of a grouse, or the cackling of a pheasant, or the splash of a duck: Through this filter of attentiveness and activity I pick up the beauty of my surroundings. The carpet of fallen leaves, more colorful and intricate than any Persian rug. The wind tossing the treetops. The way the rhododendron leaves curl in the frigid air and hang straight down like green cigars. The deep blue sky with wispy clouds. A raven kronking. The fecund smell of loam along the creek. Ice hanging in pendants and plates from trees that have toppled into the stream. But my senses are not simply resident in me: They are also out there, running with my dog. Searching, checking, testing. Through my dog, I see further, hear more sharply, scent more keenly, feel more fully the presence of game.

Jenny is now eight. At that age, I can't hunt her too many days in a row. In the field, she has started to slow down somewhat, which gets me closer shots, but it makes me sad because it reminds me she won't be with me forever. Before too long, I'll have to start thinking about another dog.

Oddly enough, I sometimes feel that one should choose a dog solely on the basis of what it looks like. That sounds like heresy. The experts all say that one should select a dog from the breed best suited to the sort of game one wants to hunt, and the way in which one will hunt it. I only know that hunting is a seeking for beauty, a beauty that is embodied in the land and the game, in the gun, and also in the dog. If a hunter's soul sings at the sight of a fleet hard-charging pointer, or a barrel-chested coal-black Lab, or a sprite of a cocker spaniel whose tail smacks it in the sides when it wags—then he or she should have one.

I have met an assortment of hunting dogs. I have encountered Chesapeake Bay retrievers lumbering bearlike through the game coverts of central Pennsylvania. I have seen, and in many cases hunted behind, Brittanys, pointers, English setters, Gordon setters, German shorthaired pointers, Labrador retrievers, golden retrievers, and American water spaniels. Once, at a public hunting area, I came upon a man who, observing Jenny, quickly bent and gathered up a gobbet of fur from the ground; he stood with his shotgun at port arms, clasping this small creature as it scrabbled against his chest and yapped at Jenny, who circled man and beast warily. It was a cockapoo. The man was hunting with a cockapoo, a cross between an American cocker spaniel and a toy poodle, both former hunting breeds now devolved into lap pets. I would have liked to watch this one in action, but it seemed too fearful of my dog.

There are many breeds that can successfully do the job of hunting. While I am not biased against any sort of dog (not even a cockapoo) that knows its task and does it well, the three basic types of bird dogs have long been the spaniels, retrievers, and pointing dogs.

The spaniels flush the game birds, hustle them into the air for the gun. They work thick cover willingly and are natural retrievers. By temperament, they are perky and bold, occasionally mischievous, often willful. To be effective, they must stay close to the gunner so that they drive up the birds within shooting range. (In open fields, this would be twenty to thirty yards; in thick cover, ten to twenty.) Spaniels are small- to medium-size dogs, twenty-five to fifty pounds, generally of a strong, sturdy build. Of the nine breeds found in this country, four are good hunting prospects.

The English springer spaniel, like my Jenny, is the most widely available. Colored liver and white or black and white, it comes in two versions, the pet-and-show variety (big-boned, blocky, with long ears and flossy fur) and the field type (smaller and leaner, more feral-looking). To have a chance of owning a gun dog, the hunter must select from the field stock. The closely related field-bred English cocker spaniel is a bit smaller and shorter-coupled than the springer. On those occasions when Jenny's natural exuberance combines with her elongated running gear to yield a flushing grouse at thirty yards, I long for a cocker. However, in the duck marsh and the pheasant field, where the birds are big and tough and the conditions rugged, I am better served by my springer. The two other hunting spaniels that have escaped being turned into nonhunting ornamentals are the American water spaniel and the Boykin spaniel.

The retrievers are bigger, burlier dogs. Chief among them are the Labrador, Chesapeake, and golden. The sturdy Labrador comes in three colors: chocolate, yellow, and basic black. One hears more and more that Labs, like English springers, have diverged into pet stock (with undistinguished noses and little interest in birds) and field-trial specialists (high-strung, tough-minded canines designed to be trained with an electric shock collar)—which is bad news indeed. One used to be able to go get a Lab and have a good hunting dog. The Chesapeake is the biggest and the most independent of the retrievers; although more of a duck and goose dog than a performer on dry-land birds, it can and will hunt upland game. Chesapeakes are stern of demeanor, and some of them are downright nasty, apt to bite other dogs and even humans. The golden is the most spaniellike of the retrievers, biddable and good-tempered. Although the pet industry churns them out by the thousands, today it is hard to find a golden out of honest working stock. Other breeds include the flat-coated retriever and the curly-coated retriever (both basically pets and show dogs) and the Nova Scotia duck tolling retriever, rare in the United States but unsullied by fashion and a good hunter.

Most retrievers do not work thick cover as thoroughly or enthusiastically as spaniels do. Which sounds like a condemnation but really is not. With touchy birds like grouse, a less-aggressive dog may actually produce closer flushes and put more game in the bag. The best of the retrievers are past masters at fetching fowl from land or water, which, after all, is their bred-in-the-bone task.

Pointing dogs cover the ground on a far grander scale than either the spaniels or the retrievers. Their job is to reach beyond the hunter, check on widely scattered patches of game cover, find the birds, point them, and remain locked in an indicative stance until the hunter catches up. There are all sorts and grades of pointing dogs, from boot polishers that you want to kick into action, to racers who fly along in the far distance giving the appearance of migrating birds; from smallish dogs to large ones, in assorted colors, coat lengths, conformations, and temperaments. No fewer than fifteen pointing breeds can be had in North America today. The best ones, and the most commonly available, include the pointer, English setter, Brittany, and German short-haired pointer. The drahthaar, or German wirehaired pointer, is a rarer breed but a renowned hunter.

Pointing dogs handle woodcock capably. They deal with pheasants and grouse (which have the nasty habit of running off once the dogs go on point) somewhat less effectively. They have little utility in hunting for doves and ducks. Few pointing dogs retrieve very well, because the act of running down and seizing a bird runs counter to their instinct—reinforced by training—to hold point. Pointing dogs require ongoing, stringent training to be effective. With spaniels and retrievers, one can simply teach obedience to voice and whistle commands, take the dog into cover, and start hunting.

Maybe it's time to talk about the birds again and discuss the ways in which the various canine types and breeds handle them.

With mourning doves, dog work amounts mainly to retrieving: quite often difficult and strenuous retrieving. Dove hunting happens in early fall, when the heat and accompanying dry conditions make for poor scenting. Doves that fall into thick grass or standing corn can be tough even for veteran retrievers to find. Dogs must be able to "mark" (discern and remember where birds fell) and work persistently to recover the game. It helps if they are taught to take hand signals or whistle commands directing them to "blind retrieves" on game they have failed to mark.

Retrievers have the edge as dove dogs. Labradors, with their (usually) patient natures, will sit for hours, quietly waiting with the hunter; their short coats keep them cool. Spaniels are likewise good at finding and fetching doves, although many are impatient in the blind, shuffling about needlessly or sitting there whining and brooming the ground with their tails. The Boykin spaniel (its tail is docked short) and the American water spaniel both have brown coats, a natural camouflage.

Pheasants—even stocked pheasants—are notorious runners that can frustrate pointing dogs. As soon as the dog locks up on the pheasant, the bird creeps off. A smart dog learns to break point, "relocate" by following the bird, and point again. Spaniels and retrievers, on the other hand, simply try to catch the bird, which straightaway gets it into the air. It is profitable to teach a flushing dog to stop on command, so that one can keep up with it when trailing a pheasant. I have a friend whose elderly Labrador retriever is deaf, especially when she doesn't want him telling her to stop on bird scent. An adaptable sort, my friend now sizes up the terrain ahead of his dog, runs out there about ninety yards, and lets her drive the pheasant to him.

Springer spaniels are frequently labeled the perfect dog for pheasants, an unfortunate honorific because it masks the fact that springers are good at hunting the gamut of upland birds. An experienced springer will get on a rooster's tail and put him up in a twinkling.

I remember a pheasant that Jenny flushed out of a tangle of briars and sumac. The bird towered up, I shot it (with a light grouse load out of a 20-gauge), and down it came like a sack of sand. Jenny ran to the spot, did a quick about-face, and headed past me, her nose to the ground. She finally nabbed the broken-winged bird (I hadn't seen it exiting the patch) about two hundred yards farther on. I have lost track of the number of wounded birds of all species that Jenny has recovered. If I knock a bird down, I know she will get it. It boosts my confidence as a shooter, knowing that my spaniel will bail me out if I fail to make a killing shot.

Of the upland birds, the woodcock is the easiest for a pointing dog to handle, since it holds tight and generally does not flush wild or run off even if the dog works in close. Woodcock must have a strong scent, judging from the distance at which some dogs detect them. Most pointing dogs will point a killed woodcock, helping the hunter find the bird against the groundcover with which it so spectacularly blends. The spaniels and retrievers also work woodcock avidly. Most will retrieve the shot birds, although some refuse to: Perhaps the woodcock's scent is so pungent they cannot bear to pick up the bird in their mouth.

If I hunted only woodcock and grouse, I think I would have a cocker spaniel. The name "cocker" derives from woodcock: In England, in centuries past, the breed became known as the "'cocking spaniel" because it was so perfectly suited to this smallish upland bird. (Each fall, the British Isles are visited by the European woodcock, midway in size between our smaller North American woodcock and our ruffed grouse.) Here in the Eastern uplands, the cocker, with its compact size, can worm and punch its way through blowdowns, willow clumps, rose tangles, and blackberry patches, favorite woodcock haunts. Since it is short-legged, in more open country the cocker must perforce stay closer to the gun than the springer.

Grouse, I have read, were once even more oafish and trusting than woodcock. Enterprising rural people shot them by the barrelful and sold them to the cities as meat. The market hunter was succeeded, early in this century, by the sport hunter with his flat cap, his plus fours, his Reo touring car, his double-barreled shotgun, and his pointing dog; ever and always his pointing dog, as extolled in books such as William Harnden Foster's *New England Grouse Shooting*, published in 1947.

Foster championed the English setter and the pointer as "real grouse dogs," bemoaned the passing of Irish and Gordon setters as working dogs, barely mentioned the Brittany and German shorthair (they had only recently appeared in the United States)—and said nothing at all about retrievers and spaniels. I agree with Foster when he writes, "Grouse hunting without a dog is not grouse hunting at all." Were he alive today, hunting in the coverts of the East and encountering the grouse as it has currently evolved, I think Foster would give a nod to the flushing dog. He might not like it—not being able to view the setter staunch on point, its banner tail hoisted—but at least he would acknowledge the effectiveness of a flushing-and-retrieving dog on a bird that now seems almost paranoic in the way that it runs and flushes wildly in avoidance of hunters and dogs.

A friend of mine pursued grouse and woodcock with English setters and pointers for many years. He also campaigned his dogs in field trials and was a judge in the trials. Today he has a Labrador retriever and a springer spaniel, and has cleaned out his kennels of other breeds. He tells me that he loves the joyous spontaneity of a dog rushing in to drive a bird from cover, along with the keenness of having to be ready to shoot at any moment. He professes to enjoy hunting much more than he did in the past. He says, "My gut feeling is that if you can keep a flushing dog close and under control, you will have the edge on most pointing dogs." He confirms my impression that, for a hunter to kill a grouse over a point, everything has to be perfect. The dog has to work perfectly; the grouse has to cower uncharacteristically. Pointing dogs, my friend says, "keep coming unglued. Every so often, they forget what they've learned and start bumping bird after bird. The training is never over."

We come now to ducks: The best dogs for hunting them are unquestionably the retrievers. The Chesapeake will actually dive after a wounded duck and pursue it underwater. The Labrador is a good compromise between a dedicated waterfowler, like the Chessie, and a breed more suited to the uplands, such as the golden. Labs can handle chill water better than most spaniels can. Among the latter, the American water spaniel is an excellent duck dog that is also a fine performer on doves, pheasants, woodcock, and grouse. Smaller and lighter than the retrievers, spaniels are handy for working out of a canoe, which is a wonderfully furtive and productive way of hunting ducks. For a dash of early-autumn ducking, with a greater emphasis on dry-land birds, I have found the English springer spaniel to be more than adequate.

When the time comes, I will probably get another springer. I might have one brought over from England: The dogs there seem somewhat less intense than their American counterparts, easier to keep in close, quieter and calmer when told to settle. The British breed dogs that are "softer," temperamentally more inclined to remain under control: Often, in Britain, springers are employed to drive pheasants toward stationary shooters (this is the well-known driven-bird shooting, as much a business venture as a sport, conducted on estates all over the British Isles), and a dog that runs amuck, and wild-flushes dozens of birds all at once, simply is not tolerated. Then again, I might go for a cocker. (Really, a good three-quarters of my hunting is for grouse and woodcock. And I have no doubt that a cocker could bring in a wood duck with ease.) I suppose that the danger in having another springer is that I would inevitably compare it with Jenny, and it might come up short.

Recently I got a letter from an upland hunter looking for a field-bred English springer pup. He asked for breeders' names and emphasized that he did not want a "field-trial hellion." I know what he meant; before we made our compromises and achieved an understanding of how we must work together, my Jenny could easily have been labeled one.

Competition has reared its head in many aspects of the field sports, but nowhere more obviously than in the breeding of dogs. On the one hand, breeders of field-trial canines have kept hunting instincts alive in many breeds. On the other hand, they have developed, in almost every case, dogs that are more intense and excitable—and therefore harder to train and control—than is needed for actual hunting.

The perfect dog for me would be Jenny, with about eighty percent of her range and drive. Hunting with Jenny, I never feel like I am just taking a walk in nature—and sometimes that's all I care to do, with a convivial dog at my side, lazing along with the possibility of flushing a bird and getting a shot or two. No, I must keep alert at all times. If Jenny gets on a hot trail and I fail to notice, she will flush the bird wild and then sprint after it, perhaps bumping other even-more-distant birds. Sometimes she is fiery beyond all reason (even at the age of eight, especially in the height of the season if I haven't hunted her for a few days). When that happens, I yell at her, take up a stick, and flog the ground beside her. Maybe she thinks she's getting a beating, or maybe she suspects I am temporarily addled and a bit dangerous, because she usually settles down and pays proper attention.

It is not easy for an amateur trainer to instill control in a dog out of field-trial lines, be it a springer, Labrador, or English setter. The trials people want dogs, as I have heard them put it, that are "always on the edge of control." The dogs that win in competition—and are subsequently used for breeding—are the dogs that run hard and fast and dramatically. Usually they compete in cover bearing little resemblance to the places where wild birds are found: The judge needs to watch the dog, and the spectators want to see what's going on, so trials are held on flat terrain, in sparse grass, on smooth-banked ponds—not in mountainside grape tangles or red-brush thickets or cattail marsh.

It is true that you can take a high-powered dog and rein it in, whereas you can never kindle the desire to hunt in a dog that lacks it in the first place. But it would be better if hunters designed the breeds they use. It is perhaps understandable why they do not. Many former hunters find themselves living in places where they cannot hunt, suburbs that are miles from any pheasants, woodcock, or grouse. They satisfy the urge to hunt by training their dogs, by getting together with like-minded people and working their dogs on pigeons and pen-reared pheasants. In the end, not enough hunters are willing to go to the trouble of breeding dogs, creating a pool of dogs whose behavior and intensity levels are tuned to the requirements of the hunt. We leave that task to the field triallers, and must adapt to what they give us.

Last autumn a man wanted to hunt with Jenny and me. He stopped at our house en route from upstate New York—where one of his two English springer spaniels had just earned a placement in a prestigious field trial—to his home in Ohio.

He could hunt for only one day, and it turned out to be rainy. We tried his spaniels, one at a time, on woodcock. Each quartered back and forth through the dripping goldenrod and brambles beneath the dense crabapple and locust trees; each keenly explored the cover, turning instantly whenever her master shrilled two pips on his whistle. The dogs flushed several woodcock, but we did not manage to shoot any of them. When the rain stepped up, we retired to the house for lunch and to talk about dogs.

By late afternoon, the rain had ended. The wind swung around to the north. Rents appeared in the clouds, and the slanting light gleamed on the rain-darkened treetrunks. I figured that the grouse, having sheltered in pines and hemlocks all day, would now be out feeding, filling their crops before nightfall. We had not hunted with Jenny yet, and now was the time.

A covert just over the hill from home, a hollow filled with brushy cutover woods. The leaves lay sodden underfoot. My companion followed his springer, I mine. Although the dogs were of similar breeding, their hunting techniques differed. My friend's dog ran in the hard, flat pattern that is rewarded in the field trials, quartering sharply, almost mechanically, her nose held high for body scent. By comparison, Jenny looked slow. She flowed through the cover, her movements intense but controlled. When quartering, she lacked the other dog's precision and snap: Instead, she coursed from one likely looking patch of brush to another, her nose to the ground, sniffing over the rocks, beneath the coils of grapevine, on the tops of logs.

I saw her take scent: the momentary pause, the lashing tail, the body low and feral as she worked out the line and followed it toward a grape tangle. I pipped on my own whistle—a single blast—and she halted in a quivering crouch.

Hastily I got into position, upslope from the twisted vines. I gave a soft double-note on the whistle, and into the tangle Jenny plunged. The grouse clattered out, right to left and angling uphill. At my shot, the bird crumpled. She was on it quickly, hitching it up in her mouth and bringing it back.

Joining my companion, I showed him the bird. It was a male (revealed by the long tail, subtle markings on the feathers of the lower back, and a reddish cast to the skin above the eye), and a bird of the year (discernible in the wear and tear on the two terminal wing primaries). We fanned the reddish-brown tail and admired the iridescent green-black shoulder ruffs. Then, with daylight fading, we swung around through the bottom of the covert and hunted back toward the car. My friend's spaniel was working closer to him now; finally she came in almost to heel. Trial dogs are accustomed to going at full tilt for brief periods, and this bitch, although a fine performer and in excellent condition, was perhaps confused at being allowed to run freely for more than a few minutes.

We were spread out, my partner and his dog to the right, Jenny looping out to the left and swinging back in toward the gun. Neither dog actually flushed the grouse: It must have felt trapped in the pincers movement we were unknowingly executing. It flew straight up (an unusual move for a grouse), cleared the trees, and hurtled back over my head. I swung my barrels upward and shot with my body extended beyond the vertical, leaning back to catch the bird in the pattern. Down it came with a thump. Jenny fetched.

The field trial man was impressed. (*I* was impressed. I think it was the second time in my life that I had killed two grouse with two shots in under ten minutes, a fact I did not bother sharing.) The second grouse was also a male, another bird of the year, quite likely from the same brood as the first. By now the sun was below the ridge; I pouched the grouse, and we finished our hunt. Back at the car, my companion snapped a flash picture of Jenny, me, and the birds. He nodded at the grouse, a rueful half-smile on his lips. "I've got a yellow ribbon," he said, referring to the prize he had won at the field trial. "You've got a brace of grouse."

3

THE GUN

Gough Thomas was an Englishman and a professional engineer so smitten with shotguns that he once rigged up a device to measure a gun's "moment of inertia," the value that best expresses its liveliness and handling qualities. He fitted a cradle with a spirit level and suspended it from the ceiling on a high-tensile steel wire. He would place a gun in this cradle, slide it forward or backward until it was level, secure it, and then make it pivot from side to side, recording with a stopwatch the time it took to complete a given number of oscillations. The shorter the time, the less energy was required to direct the gun, and the lower its "moment of inertia": The better balanced it was.

Thomas published many technical articles on shotguns from the nineteen sixties to the nineteen eighties; yet his interest was not solely in guns for their own sake. He once wrote, "Guns are fascinating things, but they are only a means to an end": For him, the sport of shooting came first, dogs and dog-work second, the guns themselves third—albeit a necessary third.

One day, Thomas and four companions were on a partridge shoot in the Hampshire Downs. They took lunch sitting against a hay rick and enjoying the bucolic scenery, the spire of Salisbury's famous cathedral on the horizon, pale against a blue September sky. The conversation dwelt on the morning's sport: the skillful shooting, the good dog work, the healthful exercise, the enjoying of these things in the company of friends. "Nobody mentioned the gun until I did," wrote Thomas later. "What about the pleasure of having a good gun in your hands?" he asked. He was met with bland comments and blank stares. Somewhat nettled, he blurted out, "Are you fellows so infernally civilized that you take no pleasure in owning and using a fine, personal weapon?"

I do take such pleasure: I hunt for doves, pheasants, woodcock, and grouse using a pair of side-by-side English game guns, one of them a 12 gauge (or 12 "bore," as Gough Thomas would have put it) and the other a 16. I shoot ducks with a modern American 12-gauge over-and-under.

When I bought my first decent shotgun twenty years ago, I chose without hesitation a side-by-side, an Ithaca SKB in 20 gauge. I may be stretching things a bit when I call it a decent gun. Made for Ithaca by a Japanese company, it was lightweight, looked pretty, and had a straight-hand stock and classic lines. Only later did I discover that it had been cheaply made (the stock split after a few years) and falsely tarted up (a fancy wood "grain" had been stained onto a plain and porous piece of walnut). When

I learned more about shotguns, I discovered to my chagrin that the little Ithaca's stock was "cast on" (angled to the left when viewed from above), for a lefthanded shooter. For me, a right-hander, this arrangement sent my shots to the left of the target. I needed a stock that was cast *off*, with the stock angling to the right, to align my right, and master, eye with the top rib so the gun would shoot exactly where I was looking. At one point, I had a brace of the SKBs—a 12 along with the 20, both of them inexplicably cast on.

I am lucky (my wife might choose a different adjective) to have a friend and gunning partner whose evolving appreciation of shotguns paralleled my own. I got an inexpensive education watching Carl buy and trade, go through firearms that seemed to both of us, at the time, to be the epitome of bird guns—old Ithacas, a Parker 12 gauge, several Winchester Model 21s, a handsome C-grade Fox 16—only to realize that other shotguns were more effective in the field and finer objects of the gunmakers' art. It was Carl who introduced me to English guns. There is truth to the saying that once you shoot an English gun, there is no going back. Last year, I flew across the Atlantic and bought two of them.

I cannot extol a hunter who buys a fancy gun just to show it off. I cannot dismiss a hunter who uses a beat-up pump, shoots it well and kills cleanly. But I think that the latter misses a certain sweet feeling of dynamism and connection that a good gun can impart.

Many hunters use pump-action or semiautomatic shotguns

in the uplands. These repeaters remind me more of military ordnance than of sporting arms. I dislike the clashing sounds they make. They are efficient in a mechanical sense, although, like automatic windows in a car, they are complicated and more prone to misbehave than the simpler double-barrel design. They deliver three shots, certainly, but two are almost always enough.

Nor is a repeater as safe as a double: If I stop to chat with someone in the coverts, I can open my gun's barrels and demonstrate that the piece cannot go off by accident. Years ago, I shot at a woodcock, and heard a *phoosh* and then the pellets raining weakly on the brush; the 'cock flew ahead and landed, and I quickly reloaded and went after it. Then I stopped. I opened my gun, removed the cartridge from the right barrel, and looked down the tube. There, about halfway along, was the plastic wad left by the dud round. Had my gun not been so easy to open— had I been carrying a repeater, which cannot be easily dismantled in the field—I might not have taken the time to check it. I might have flushed the woodcock, pulled the trigger—and lost a barrel, and perhaps my left hand.

The reasons for wanting a double gun go beyond safety. Because of the way its weight centers between the shooter's hands, a well-made double will handle more fluidly than a semiautomatic or a pump, which, with its longer action and extended magazine tube, will have its weight too far forward.

Once the hunter decides to have a double gun, dozens of factors must be considered. Gauge. The gun's weight and balance. The shooter's own size and physical strength. Conditions in the hunting coverts. A preference among game birds: pheasants over grouse, for example. Cost. Barrel length, stock profile and dimensions, type of action, two triggers or one, choking, location of the safety. . . .

Generally the first decision is whether to have an over-and-under or a side-by-side. To me a side-by-side looks sleeker than an over-and-under. I particularly fancy a slim, straight-hand stock (no bulbous pistol grip to interrupt the sweep of the wood from butt to action) and a splinter fore-end; with them, the gun has no excess flesh on its bones.

The combination of a straight stock and a minimalist fore-end places the hands on the same plane as the gun itself, so that the shot passes directly from the hands to the target. A pistol grip combined with a beavertail fore-end also puts the hands on the same plane, but one that is fractionally lower than the plane of the bores. I think I *aim* an over-and-under better (perhaps explaining why I shoot mine fairly well on clay targets, which have a predictable flight), but *direct* a side-by-side more instinctively when shooting at feathered birds.

Gauge is a matter of personal preference. With the exception of distant ducks and pheasants, the birds of the Eastern uplands can be killed cleanly and consistently with an ounce of shot. The 12 gauge, 16 gauge, and 20 gauge all can deliver an ounce. Of the three, the 12 has the best chance of shooting that ounce in an even pattern (with fewer bird-sized gaps in it). The natural load for the 20 is $\frac{7}{8}$ ounce; a full ounce of shot, piled high in the 20's skinny cartridge, may throw a patchier pattern compared to the two larger bores. The 28 gauge, which standardly shoots $\frac{3}{4}$ ounce, can make a useful grouse and woodcock gun in the hands of one who eschews long shots and regularly centers the target; however, the 28 is too light for pheasants and ducks and only marginally adequate for grouse. Overloaded with an ounce of shot, the 28 may perform poorly.

A handy thing about a 12 gauge is that it can efficiently shoot $1\frac{1}{16}$-ounce and $1\frac{1}{8}$-ounce loads, making it more versatile than the 16 or the 20; and the 12 can also be loaded down to $\frac{7}{8}$ ounce. Then there is the matter of recoil. In general, the heavier the powder and shot charges, the more a gun will "kick." The lighter the gun, the less recoil it will absorb and the more it will pass on to the shooter. The trick is to use a gun heavy enough to dampen recoil, yet light enough to be carried comfortably and handled with alacrity.

The typical American 12 gauge weighs seven to eight pounds, usually closer to the second figure. The average American 16 weighs six and a half to seven pounds. The average American 20 weighs a few ounces over six pounds, even up to seven pounds in some models. American guns are sometimes scorned for being excessively heavy, but there is a reason for their heft. In England, the government long ago passed strict laws under which all shotgun barrels must be proven capable of safely firing specific loads: generally, $1\frac{1}{8}$ ounces of shot for the 12 bore, 1 ounce for the 16, and $\frac{7}{8}$ ounce for the 20, fired from $2\frac{1}{2}$-inch cartridges (as opposed to the American standards of $2\frac{3}{4}$ and 3 inches) propelled by a gunpowder charge generating a moderate chamber pressure. American manufacturers (and European and Asian makers eyeing the U.S. market) do not have—and never have had—such proof laws to which they can adhere. Instead, they must build firearms capable of withstanding whatever shot and powder charge the most power-hungry shooter crams into them: In 12 gauge, a 2¾-inch shell loaded with 1½ ounces of shot, or even a 3-inch shell with 2¼ ounces, backed by sufficient propellant to send the pellets zipping along at thirteen hundred or so feet per second. Loads of this sort have little or no utility for the upland hunter who nevertheless must tote around a shotgun stout enough to fire them without flying into pieces.

I am of a size that thirty years ago would have been considered "average" and today perhaps is classifiable as "small." (Someone interviewing me for a magazine once characterized me as "slight," which sounded dismissive.) I am five feet, nine inches, and weigh one hundred forty-five pounds. (Make that "lean" or "wiry," please.) My English 12, at six pounds, five ounces, suits me nicely; my English 16, at just six pounds, seems even more appropriate to my frame and approaches the perfect weight for a grouse and woodcock gun. My American over-and-under, a Ruger 12 gauge, weighs seven pounds, twelve ounces. The Ruger balances well and soaks up recoil. Although designed for shooting clay targets, it excels in the duck blind and is usable for jump shooting, although I wouldn't want to haul it through the grouse brush all day.

The Ruger's barrels are thirty inches. Those long tubes help me swing through a passing claybird or a duck, but in covert they are slow to get into action. During the last century, barrels of thirty and thirty-two inches were the standard, necessary for the full combustion of blackpowder propellant. When smokeless gunpowder was invented, barrel length could be reduced, since combustion occurred much more rapidly. It took decades to happen, but gun manufacturers finally began making barrels shorter, yielding shotguns that were lighter and livelier.

Today, some observers believe the trend toward short barrels has gone too far. (Don't most trends work that way?) In England, a popular length is twenty-five inches. Here, twenty-six inches is common. Short-barreled guns have their drawbacks, though. They look odd in the hands of large people. In 12 gauge, they have a stubby appearance. More important, short barrels do not show up as obviously in the shooter's vision, making a short-barreled gun more difficult to point accurately than a long-barreled gun. Although easier to get moving, short barrels are harder to keep in motion, to keep swinging with the target, necessary for consistent wingshooting success. And when fired, they are noticeably louder than long barrels, distracting the shooter and damaging his or her hearing. My English 12 bore has twenty-seven-inch barrels, which seems a reasonable compromise for the uplands. Twenty-eight-inch barrels likewise are very fine, especially when mated to light-framed 16- or 20-bore guns.

Certain shotguns, when you pick them up, feel "sweet": They leap to the shoulder and can be pointed swiftly and surely in different directions. As mentioned at the outset of this chapter, Gough Thomas, the English writer and engineer, invented a device for measuring shotgun balance. The best-balanced firearm he tested was a 12-bore side-by-side having twenty-seven-inch barrels and weighing six pounds, three ounces. (He doesn't say, but I suspect it was his own personal gun, made to his specifications by the London firm of Henry Atkin in 1948.) An Italian automatic and a well-known Italian over-and-under each possessed a much higher moment of inertia, showing, Thomas wrote, "how far certain popular guns fall short of the standards of balance, liveliness, and fast-handling that have been attained by the best guns hitherto made in this country." Thomas confirmed that in the best-balanced shotguns the majority of the weight is concentrated between the shooter's hands—neither biased toward the buttstock nor the barrels, but between the appendages that move and direct the gun. Other factors he cited as adding to the overall sensation of good balance were "fluent lines," "well-finished surfaces," and a shape that was "conformable to the hand and pleasant to the sense of touch."

In Thomas's opinion, the fastest-handling guns (light ones having twenty-five-, twenty-six-, or twenty-seven-inch barrels) "show at their best at such sport as partridge driving or rabbit, pigeon, or woodcock shooting in covert," while the slowest-handling guns (heavier ones with thirty-inch barrels) "are least disadvantageous, or, it may be, positively advantageous, for duck flighting and the like."

There are two main types of double-barreled shotgun actions: the boxlock and the sidelock. The sidelock, an older design, is somewhat more exacting and expensive to make. Its operating mechanisms, or locks (as in "lock, stock, and barrel"), attach to the insides of flat metal plates, which in turn are fitted to the sides of the firearm. These side plates, bounded above and below by the stock wood, provide a goodly surface for decorative engraving. The sidelock's trigger pulls are said to be slightly smoother than those of the boxlock. (I can't tell any difference.)

Unlike the boxlock, the sidelock design commonly incorporates "intercepting sears," which prevent the gun from firing should it be jarred, as by being dropped on the ground.

The boxlock is a simpler concept. Invented in Birmingham, England, in 1875 by the gunsmiths William Anson and John Deeley, it requires less-complicated inletting of the stock wood to accept the action. It can be made lighter, having less steel in its mechanism. It is more resistant to water seeping in. These attributes did not prevent, in 1896, the famous English game shot Sir Ralph Payne-Gallwey from pronouncing the boxlock shotgun a "monstrous horrendum," "a mere unwieldy log of iron and wood when compared to the perfect article produced in London." To this day in England it is more prestigious to be seen shooting a London-built sidelock (most boxlocks were made in Birmingham), showing that snobbishness is alive and well on the Scepter'd Isle. In the United States, vintage side-by-sides of boxlock design include the Parker, Fox, Ithaca, Lefever, and Winchester Model 21; the current crop of over-and-unders also are boxlocks. The famous L. C. Smith was a sidelock (although it lacked intercepting sears).

Some older American side-by-sides—and almost all British game guns—have two triggers. Double triggers are simpler and less apt to malfunction than single triggers. They offer an instant choice of choke, taking full advantage of the double-barrel design. In the classic side-by-side, the front trigger shoots the right barrel, traditionally having an open choke (cylinder or improved cylinder) to fire a wide swarm of shot at a bird at short range. The left barrel possesses a greater degree of choke (quarter, modified, improved modified, or full), yielding a pattern that is tighter—and therefore more lethal—at longer ranges. The normal sequence is to first shoot the open barrel; then, if the bird is missed, to follow with the choke. But sometimes a bird gets up at a distance—thirty or forty yards, say—so that one wants the tighter barrel for what will be the only shot taken. On a gun with two triggers, it is a simple matter to slide the hand back and pull the rear trigger to instantly fire the tighter choke. A straight-hand stock (as opposed to a pistol grip) facilitates this movement by the trigger hand, either to fire the choke barrel first, or to fire the open and then the choke in the usual sequence.

Today, almost all factory-made shotguns come equipped with single triggers. Usually there is a complicated safety button mounted on the top tang that can be thumbed in one direction to select the open barrel, in the other direction to select the choke. The people in the marketing departments of firearms companies, most of whom obviously have never seen the inside of a thorn-apple thicket or an alder swamp, want us to believe that a selective safety is easy to operate during the heat of a flush. It is not. About the only time a single trigger outperforms double triggers is during frigid weather when a stationary hunter (sitting in a duck blind, for instance) loses feeling in his or her fingers. Both of my English guns have two triggers; I had never shot double triggers before getting them, but reckoned that if I could learn to drive on the left side of the road (over a thousand miles while shopping for guns), I could teach myself to use two triggers. I could, and did, and it didn't take very long.

After I got shut of my SKBs, I thought long and hard

about what kind of gun I wanted. It had to be well-balanced and dynamic, for those snap shots on grouse. It had to carry easily, for the long treks over hill and dale. A gun whose beauty would make me want to get it out and look at it, pick it up and handle it, shoot it often. As I saw it, there were three possible avenues for procuring an excellent upland gun.

The first route—by far the simplest and the most practical—was to buy a modern high-quality shotgun. A host of over-and-under boxlocks are manufactured by American, European, and Asian makers. Most are priced at around a thousand dollars (secondhand ones are less) and offer considerable value for the money. They are chambered for cartridges of the standard 2¾- or 3-inch lengths. Many come with interchangeable choke tubes that let the shooter set up the choke combination for the birds and the cover conditions at hand.

Most modern over-and-unders can safely shoot steel shot, currently mandated for hunting ducks. Most of these shotguns are predictably heavy, steering the average shooter toward the 20 rather than the 12 gauge. As far as I can tell, no one makes a 16, which is a shame because the 16 is lighter and trimmer than the 12 and can handle both upland birds and ducks: The 20 is a bit underpowered for shooting waterfowl. I know of no company that makes a good-quality, modestly priced side-by-side, probably because American shooters overwhelmingly prefer over-and-unders.

A normal fellow would have chosen a modern gun. But remember, I had handled Carl's English.

For a while I considered getting an older American side-by-side. These guns hold a treasured place in the hearts of many shooters; they hearken back to what is imagined to be a simpler time, when game was more abundant and a predominantly rural populace held the sport of bird hunting in higher regard than does today's urbanized society. In 12 gauge (the most common gauge then, as now), most of the old Yankee guns are clunky: heavy, thick through the wrist, with pistol grips and wrap-around beavertail fore-ends. I handled many such at gun shows and in shops. Perhaps, I thought, I could be happy with a 16 or a 20.

Mass-produced in factories, most of the vintage American guns did not receive the care and craftsmanship invested in English and European doubles, handwork that resulted in sleek lines, subtle adornment, and good balance. Despite any negative qualities, old American doubles—especially those in original condition—command high prices. Parker shotguns, for example, seem absurdly expensive, as do Winchester Model 21s, especially compared with English guns available at a similar cost.

The higher grades of the American doubles can be downright gaudy. Various models sport checkered side panels, *fleurs de lis* carved into the stock wood, and even gold lightning bolts inlaid in the barrels. The engraving is often copious, although much of it is imprecise, and some of the dogs and birds suggest that Dr. Seuss was manning the engraving tool. To me, the lower grades look better—the V Grade Parker and Fox Sterlingworth, for example, their actions outlined with modest border engraving—and, happily, these simpler guns cost less than the high-grade ones. It would be possible, although not easy, to find an old American double with two triggers and a straight stock.

It is also an option to have a gun restocked to modern dimensions.

But really, my case was hopeless. New books had accumulated on my shelves, such as *Gough Thomas's Gun Book* and Geoffrey Boothroyd's *Sidelocks & Boxlocks, the Classic British Shotguns.* Little yellow stick-on markers feathered the back issues of magazines featuring fine guns. I visited toney gun-trading establishments and emerged in a state combining agony and ecstasy. I wrote to English companies for lists. I struck up an over-the-phone friendship with a man who had lived in England and who had bought many shotguns there, for himself and for friends. It was clear that English guns cost considerably less in England than they did here. It was complicated, bringing them over, but it could be done. From my new friend, and from Carl and through my reading, I learned of certain considerations regarding English shotguns: Like the older American doubles, they were not built to handle steel shot. Most English guns have 2½-inch chambers that will not accept the 2¾-inch shells found in sporting goods shops in the United States. The solution was to buy imported English cartridges (at about twice the cost of American ammunition) or, as I planned to do, reload your own.

I had incurably caught what I sometimes jokingly referred to as "the shotgun bane." Only an English gun would relieve it.

The English game gun is the ultimate evolutionary expression of the side-by-side shotgun. It is as lean as it can be made, and still remain comfortable to shoot. While many English doubles have magnificent stock wood and superb engraving, their beauty does not depend on applied adornment. Scheming after my gun, I realized I could be happy with a twin-triggered, light-weight firearm with little or no metal engraving and plain stock wood: Such a gun still sings out its correctness of form. Gough Thomas had coined a word to describe the best of the English guns, *eumatic*, meaning "the quality in a manually operated device whereby it is totally correlated to the human being who [uses] it."

At that juncture, a fortunate thing happened. Years earlier, I had squirreled away some old sporting art. I learned that the art had value, and sold it. Now I had dollars burning holes in my pockets. Enough dollars, it would seem, for two guns: a plain one and a fancy. The British pound had sunk to one dollar and fifty cents. I pointed out to my wife that the value of English shotguns had steadily risen and would continue to do so. Sidelocks were quite expensive, but boxlocks—so the experts said—remained underpriced. I managed to convince my wife that I was turning one form of investment (the artwork) into another, eminently more usable, form of investment (the guns). And hadn't she always wanted to visit England?

We flew in April. London was rain, traffic, crowds—and places like Holland & Holland and Purdeys, where sleek, gorgeous sidelocks lined the racks, most of them (even the used ones) costing upwards of ten thousand pounds. No doubt about it, boxlocks were the bargains, and I would find them in the countryside.

Spring was just coming on. Outside the city, fruit trees were in blossom, lambs frolicked across kelly-green meadows, and the mustard fields were brilliant yellow coverlets spread on the fertile earth. Our first stop was seventy miles southwest of the metropolis, in the town of Chichester. The proprietor of Chichester Armoury was a sandy-haired, quiet-spoken gent whose John Hancock was ... John Hancock. The shop, on West Street not far from the town's imposing Norman cathedral, smelled of gun oil, waxed cotton, and wool. Outside, the rain spattered down, and inside I happily laid my hands on some guns.

I looked at boxlocks and sidelocks, ordinary and dressy, cheap and dear. Finally I picked up the gun that had drawn me to the shop in the first place. (We had also gone to Chichester because it was on the way from London to Cornwall, where my wife, son, and I would be vacationing for two weeks. At the moment, they were enjoying themselves at Chichester Cathedral.)

The gun was a 16-bore boxlock made in the nineteen thirties by George Hinton of Taunton, Somerset. Taunton is a town in the west of England, in Somerset, which is a "shire," similar to our "county" designation. Hinton was one of many "provincial" gunmakers whose businesses were located outside of London. (One source book lists four thousand gunmakers, or firms that sold shotguns under their own name: In actuality, most boxlocks were made anonymously in shops and factories in Birmingham.) The 16 was not a fancy gun but an honest one—a "bramble divider," as the English call a firearm destined for hard use. It had its share of nicks and scratches, so I wouldn't be afraid to carry it on icy slopes or through the wickedest briars. At six pounds, I could carry it all day and still get onto a grouse flushed in the waning light. The price, twelve hundred fifty pounds, included a leather case and the reblacking of the barrels, trigger guard, and floorplate.

"Done," I said.

Mr. Hancock noted that he had sold the Hinton through his shop five years earlier, the buyer having traded it back in on a rifle. He smiled, hefting the little double. "I don't expect to own it again," he said.

I found my 12 bore in Salisbury, whose cathedral spire had caught Gough Thomas's eye on that September day of partridge shooting. It was market day when we arrived; in the town square, people sold fresh produce, rugs, fabric, shoes, eggs, butchered meat. When I walked into Greenfields, I knew it was my kind of place. Plenty of doubles on the racks—stacked-barrel Browning and Beretta clays guns—but also a fine complement of English side-by-sides. Richard Moore, in green gunmaker's smock, white shirt, and tie, oversaw the gun room. He had a countryman's genial face below a shock of gray-streaked brown hair.

I looked at several guns—a Wanless Brothers, a Newnham, a couple of Gallyons, a Martin, a Stensby—all 12 bores, none of them names that I knew, but obviously well-made boxlock game guns, most of them in excellent condition and priced between twelve hundred and three thousand pounds. Forget the names, this is what you look for: good lines, high quality, top condition.

Then I came to the Rosson.

The moment I picked it up, the gun felt at home in my hands. Its light weight resided perfectly about the hinge pin. It came to my shoulder swiftly, stayed there, could be quickly and positively redirected. The stock fit me perfectly. Again and again, I swept the gun to my shoulder, then lowered it and turned it in my hands. English ivy carved impeccably into the fences. A partridge engraved on the floorplate and another on the top lever; fine scrollwork on the action, trigger guard, top and bottom tangs, and fore-end furniture. The metallic blues, reds, greens, and purples of antique case-coloring swirled across the surface of the action. Black lines played through the richly colored French walnut stock.

The Rosson had been made in the nineteen thirties by the now-defunct firm of C. S. Rosson & Company (their address, "Rampant Horse Street, Norwich," was engraved on the top rib). By chance, Mr. Moore had a Rosson catalog from the thirties, which identified the gun as a "Regent" model, their top-of-the-line boxlock. Back then, it cost forty-seven pounds, ten shillings, just five pounds less than their lowest-priced sidelock. (That was at a time when the average English workman made five to ten pounds a month.) Of the Regent, C. S. Rosson & Company stated: "Particular attention is paid to Weight and Balance, and the Gun is a perfect delight to use."

The Rosson was just within my budget. It is a better gun than any old American double I have ever seen. It is a better gun than some English sidelocks costing several thousand pounds more. Indeed, it has proven a perfect delight to use, here in the uplands of Pennsylvania.

I suppose I am odd for going all the way to England to buy my guns. But we had a memorable trip, and I refuse to count the journey's cost into the price of the guns—which admittedly was

considerable. My wife thinks I am insane for buying two shotguns whose combined worth is twice that of my pickup truck.
Yes, an English game gun is expensive. But the weight is right,
the profile classic, and the balance superb. How correct it seems
to pursue birds with a firearm as honed and lovely as they.

4

B ALANCE

I am hunting for something just now: the reasons why I hunt.

The reasons reside in the land, and in me. I can get nearer them by following the dog. I cannot bag them with the shotgun—but carrying and shooting a fine gun, an effective gun, brings me closer to comprehending the full matter, stating the difficult equation.

I believe hunters owe it to themselves to try to understand what it is that urges them out. To fail to examine the source of the hunting instinct is to fail to experience it fully. It is too simple to say it is good exercise, or pleasant pastime, or exciting sport, or even a means of experiencing nature. It is these things and more; it is about learning to be patient, giving thanks, becoming a child again. It is about facing death, and living life, and participating in the present as fully as one can.

I had my shotgun over my arm, my whistle, on its lanyard, around my neck. Jenny and I crossed the meadow and entered the woods. We hiked to Oak Pond Hollow. When I built my house ten years ago, the hollow was being logged; the old township road, used as a skid by the loggers, remains a trail through the new growth of aspen, maple, and oak.

Blackberry canes arced beneath the saplings; grapevines with their flaky brown bark curled and corkscrewed from the ground up into the trees. Trotting fluently through the brush, Jenny took scent. The butt of my shotgun was tucked between my elbow and side, ready to slip to my shoulder. A brown stuttering blur that banked: a grouse flushing wild. I marked its flight and followed. We threaded through mountain laurel, passed stumps sprouting deer-browsed stems. We crossed a trickle of water. Jenny paused, lashing her tail. I was heart-poundingly ready: Often a grouse will hold tighter after having once been flushed.

I let my eyes rove, slightly unfocused, to seize on any movement. My ears listened for wings flapping or the *pert-pert* call of a nervous grouse. The spaniel darted into a laurel patch—and the grouse drummed out the other side. The shotgun sought the prey. The bird, a large male, flashed behind a three-trunked oak. It veered, keeping the tree-clump between itself and me; and I did not see it again, in its flight, until it was beyond shooting, climbing the ridge.

I was tempted to strike off in a new direction but decided to pursue the known bird. We worked upslope. It was slower going for me than for Jenny; I had to use the whistle to keep her in range. We reached the top and turned into the wind. After a hundred yards she showed scent. The third flush was the closest of all: The bird thundered out from behind a log. I had a quick, clear shot, and saw the right wing break, and the bird appeared to be fighting with the air as it came tumbling, fluttering down.

I lost sight of it in the underbrush as Jenny raced after.

I looked around. Deep blue sky. On the dry leaves, knife-edged shadows cast by the late autumn sun. The far mountains brownish with a faint violet tint. The air crystalline. Sweating as I was from the climb, the wind cut through me.

Back she came, her tail wagging slowly. Her ears were cupped back, and her eyes were on mine. As always, I was flooded with emotion to see this tableau of cooperation, this voluntary bringing back of the game; for me, it is the ultimate moment in the hunt. "Good girl," I murmured, kneeling to receive. The grouse had its head up. Its brown eye glittered. As Jenny slowed to let me take it, it drew back its head and drove its bill into her eye.

I clasped the bird. Pressing it against the ground with one hand, I checked the spaniel with the other; she was blinking, but her eye appeared uninjured. I picked the bird up. It kept its head level, compensating for my movements. I studied the grouse. Had it struck instinctively, as birds will, at a bright object? Had it been defending itself? Had it lashed out of its own free will, born of desperation or anger? I could read nothing in the avian face. I took the bird's head in one hand, twisted until I felt the neck snap. The death tremors seized the grouse, which shook and shuddered in my hands.

We have lost, over the millennia, a way of formally giving thanks—to the earth spirit that moves in all animals, to the bird itself. Certainly I felt no rancor toward the grouse; rather, a tinge of sadness and a sense of awe. I had always assumed that birds were creatures strictly of instinct and reaction. This cock grouse had challenged that notion. And yet I thought I would not stop hunting grouse, even if I believed them sentient.

I could have thanked God. Maybe I did, for I remained kneeling with the bird in my hands, studying the colors and runes of its plumage; its short, down-turned beak, now slacked open; the membranous eyelids that were slowly curtaining up, reptilian fashion, from beneath. As occasionally happens, a louse fly crawled out of the bird's breast feathers: a squat, plated, dun-colored, inch-long parasite that flitted from its haven (Had it sensed a slight cooling?) to buzz in my face; I shooed it away; and off it flew into the chilly woods, to what I supposed was its own imminent demise.

People have hunted since before they were people. They hunted through the hundreds of thousands of years that constitute the Paleolithic age: We have found ample, widespread evidence in the spear points, tools, and the hauntingly accurate and lovely cave paintings they left behind.

Hunting is in our blood. (It is evident in our teeth: The combination of incisors, canines, and molars signal an animal that eats both meat and plant matter.) First and foremost, we were hunter-gatherers. We turned to agriculture only recently, as such things go, within the last fifteen thousand years. This change in feeding behavior allowed our species to thrive, our brains to exercise their powers, our population to expand. Better for the planet (and better for ourselves, according to at least one school of anthropological thought) had we stayed people of the hunt.

In any case, we find ourselves nearing the twenty-first century in a world of things and comforts and distractions, a world (so they tell me) of exponentially increasing knowledge and (as I see it) of dwindling wisdom. Those who study the stone-age tribes still left on earth tell of people who enjoy lives of relative ease and plenty; people who are self-possessed, sociable, mystical. There is no rat race in the depths of the Amazon, no crime on the Kalahari. When someone suggests to me that hunting is primitive, I agree. When they suggest that chasing after birds with a shotgun is a waste of time, I disagree. Primitive it is; wonderfully, urgently so. Useless in terms of productivity, perhaps, but it seems far less wasteful, less extinguishing, than time spent commuting to a job, or laboring on an assembly line, or filing away one's life, hour by hour, behind a desk.

In 1926, Henry Beston, then thirty-eight years of age, went to live in a two-room cottage he had built on Eastham Beach on the outer arm of Cape Cod. After a two-week stay, he decided to linger on because, as he put it in his long-lived book, *The Outermost House,* "the beauty and mystery of this earth and outer sea so possessed and held me that I could not go." Beston wrote, "The world today is sick to its thin blood for lack of elemental things, for fire before the hands, for water welling up from the earth, for air, for the dear earth itself underfoot."

The situation has changed little, and immensely, since Beston penned those lines. We are still sick to our thin blood for lack of elemental things. And we are shaken and riven by the knowledge that, conceived by our brains and wrought by our hands, are weapons of destruction that can expunge us from the planet. Not only us, but also the wild creatures we once mingled with and revered, who sustained us, whose spirits still link with ours even if we forget this fact in our caged and diverted lives.

Hunting is among those "elemental things," perhaps one of the most elemental. Today it has become symbolic and is generally waning. (Although not everywhere: Here in rural central Pennsylvania, many people depend on deer meat, and businesses and schools close down for certain key days in deer season.) I could go buy Cornish game hens from the supermarket in the city over the mountain. I could probably buy a lifetime supply of Cornish hens for the funds I have expended on shotguns, ammunition, vests, boots, a dog, dogfood, veterinary bills, licenses, and the gasoline burned getting to and from the game coverts. But my life would be lacking. It would lack that essential interweaving contact. It would lack an identity that I have striven toward, found, and nurtured. It would, in certain important ways, no longer be a means of paying respect.

I am not as driven, as determined in my hunting as I once was; nor as obsessed with it as some others. One of those people called me on the telephone the other evening and informed me that he had flushed five hundred and seven grouse over the course of the season. (Remember, the average is 1.5 birds per hour.) Others like to announce how many birds they have bagged, including some astonishingly high numbers: They must shoot a lot straighter than I do, have better coverts, spend more time in them, and enjoy keeping score. I shoot between twenty and thirty of the larger game birds in a season, plus a couple of dozen doves. I feel no need to kill more. In truth, I find it unsettling to be doing too much hunting; I also have identities as a husband, father, and writer. Yet it must be present, this annual autumnal focusing, this guiding activity, this reimmersion in things immediate and savage.

Hunting lets me prove my endurance. Often I have to walk many miles, earn what I kill with my legs and lungs, and be satisfied with little or nothing. I go-hunting in places I would never venture into if not in pursuit of game: Multiflora rose thickets. Willow tangles. Steep briar-ridden hillsides where the footing is chancy and the view magnificent (the valley scrolling out bluely, north and south under snow). Ice-rimmed cattail marshes where a misstep means a bone-chilling bath. Why else, if not to hunt woodcock, would I suit up in waxed cotton and rubber boots, and go out into the November rain, and muck around in alder jungles? Would I trudge through knee-deep snow into a stiff north wind if I didn't have a chance at a late-season grouse? I doubt I would endure these things to go camping, search for fossils, or take a photograph.

To hunt them well, one needs to know much about grouse and woodcock and ducks, what they feed on, where they spend the night. When I kill a bird, I slit the crop and check what it was eating. In knowing where the birds forage, and where they lay up in certain weathers, and the predators they must circumvent, I involve myself more deeply with their lives. I read about them and think about them. I am concerned with the game not only in the fall but the whole year around. To have good hunting grounds, I must ferret them out: I drive, observe, poke around in the canoe. I explore isolated hollows and winding township roads. I knock on farmhouse doors. Look for abandoned fields and the red-brush haze of cutover slopes. Read newspapers and note the locations of forest fires (in a few years, grouse will prosper in the stems that come shooting up), study topographic maps, aerial photographs, and wetlands inventories. Mostly, though, I get out and walk.

In *Pilgrim at Tinker Creek,* Annie Dillard wrote about wild animals: "They show me by their very wariness what a prize it is simply to open my eyes and behold." I would not necessarily urge Ms. Dillard to get out there with her over-and-under. But hunting those wary animals—opening one's eyes (and also one's ears and, by extension through the dog, one's nose), and striving to make a game bird appear, then beholding it (*really* beholding it: one needs to focus with double intensity when shooting) and manipulating the shotgun to down the speeding form—avails me of the greatest prize of all: At times I become so immersed in hunting that I lose track of the passage of time. I forget who and what and where I am.

In *Meditations on Hunting,* the Spanish philosopher José Ortega y Gasset described the hunter as "the alert man." Hunting, I move through and across the landscape, my senses primed, on edge. I seek out different sorts of cover as the day passes or the weather changes. I find the act of hunting to be a way of regaining and strengthening the ability to concentrate, to control my senses and intellect, to overcome fatigue. The skill of concentrating is destroyed, I believe, by the multitudinous distractions of today's world—the dross of television, billboards, radio advertisements, possessions heaped high in stores, luxurious houses, shining cars. We need rituals to keep these distractions at arm's length. Hunting, done properly, becomes such a ritual.

I rise with the sun, tread upon the earth, exercise my mind, my senses, my body. I find satisfaction even on those outings when few birds are sighted, when the bag is empty at day's end. How magnificent to stop and watch a cloud pass before the sun; pure water bubbling up from a sand spring; the twinkling gold of aspen leaves set to life by the slightest wind. How fine it is to be patient, absorbed in one's surroundings. It is enough to share these things with the dog, who injects no words but lets her avidity and love shine through her every motion.

The English author T. H. White called fishing "the only pure sport," "a secret rapture." Shooting, he said, "is mixed up with fear of the next gun, lest he should wipe your eye and kill a bigger bag—in fact, with fear of failing to excel." White was referring to the gunning of driven birds, a formal exercise conducted by an assemblage of shooters standing in a row—and not to rough shooting, the sort of hunting that I do, ranging out alone upon the land, or with one trusted partner. I never fear I will fail when hunting wild birds. It is easy to miss. There is no shame in it. And if I do miss, the bird goes free to be hunted again, which is a comforting thought.

When hunting, I need not prove anything or achieve any goal. At its best, hunting is almost like play—not careless, casual play, but important play that lets me shed my serious adult humanness and revert to being a child, an animal among animals. Hunting is for me, as fishing was for White, truly a secret rapture.

At the end of one unusually successful day, I plucked two grouse on the edge of our meadow, leaving the feet and the heads for the scavengers. My son, five years old at the time, happened upon the scatter of pretty feathers. I was working at some other task outside, and had an immediate pang when I saw him pick something up. As I approached, I saw his face knotted up. He looked at me, a grouse leg in one hand, a head in the other.

I can't remember my exact words, but we talked about killing. I told my son that whatever we do, we end up taking life. Living arises from killing, new life from the ashes of death. To eat, we are forced to kill—something. I tried to explain that even planting a field was an act that caused death, through banishment of the creatures that originally lived in the brush or the grass that was abolished to make the field. Whatever we do, I told my son, we affect the world. The pang I had felt when seeing him was sadness in knowing that he must come to an understanding of how the world functions—an understanding that includes the realization that he himself will not abide on the earth forever.

The source of our living is something that many modern people wish to keep in the background. Theirs, as T. H. White put it, is "an abstract world where water is an idea that comes out of a tap, and light a conception in a switch." And where food, I would add, is a perquisite gotten from a shelf in boxes or cans, or plastic-wrapped from a display case. At times, I have been condemned by vegetarians for my hunting. I wonder if they count the number of worms, beetles, flies, spiders, mice, rabbits, sparrows, and hawks whose habitat is destroyed by the fields of vegetables, the deserts of soybeans. I can kill a bird, then go back the next year and flush another one from the same place.

But there's no denying it: Killing is an integral part of the hunt. As the philosopher Ortega has noted, "One does not hunt in order to kill; on the contrary, one kills in order to have hunted." The whole intricate, difficult ritual comes to fruition in the moment that the prey is slain. Some have written that if they could bring down a bird without killing it, in the same manner that a fisherman can land a trout without harming it, they would never kill another. To me this sounds like an affected piety, at best a conceit not fully thought through.

Archie Carr, a naturalist from Florida, writes, "Almost from birth I have been peculiarly tormented by Jekyll-and-Hyde compulsions both to learn about the natural history of animals and to eat them." For me, no such guilt exists. Which is not to say that I do not feel an elegiac, almost a weary sadness when a bird, formerly vibrant and cunning, lies inert in my hands. But the skillful shooting exonerates the killing, as does the dog in her great joy, as does the preparing and eating of the game, themselves acts of veneration. Cleaning a bird, I marvel at the mechanics of its body, the overlay of feathers, the limbs and appendages well suited to certain modes of living (the grouse's fringed snowshoe feet and the duck's ruddering paddles, the woodcock's worm-gripping bill). Eating a bird, I savor it twice: I taste the succulent flesh, and I remember how I brought it to bag. After the meal I boil the carcass for soup. I strain out the bones and scatter them in the woods, or, if there's a hot fire in the stove, toss them in and burn them. The ash is spread on my garden in the spring.

Probably I sound more convinced than I really am in describing my feelings about killing. I am never fully certain that what I do is correct. I somehow think that doing as much of life's killing myself is better than paying someone else (whether slaughterer or farmer) to do it by proxy. Sometimes I wonder if animals have souls. My dog, I believe, has one. It would not surprise me if the grouse who drove his bill into Jenny's eye had a soul. But there is in me a savage joy that even the thought of life-taking and soul-extinguishing cannot put down. I take my chances. I kill swiftly, eat what I slay, and keep the knowledge of my own death close at hand.